2015 BASKETBALL SUPERSTARS

By K.C. Kelley

SCHOLASTIC

PHOTO CREDITS:

Photos ©: cover, left: Noah Graham/NBAE/Getty Images; cover, center: Don Kelly Photo/Corbis Images; cover, right: Tony Dejak/AP Images; p1: Larry W. Smith/AP Images; p2: Viorika/iStockphoto; p3: Paul Bersebach/The Orange County Register/Corbis Images; pp4, 5: Daniel Gluskoter/ICON SMI/Corbis Images; pp6, 7, 8, 9: Andrew D. Bernstein/NBAE/Getty Images; pp10, 11: Jonathan Bachman/AP Images; pp12, 13: Layne Murdoch/NBAE/Getty Image; pp14, 15: Larry W. Smith/AP Images; pp16, 17: Paul Bersebach/The Orange County Register/Corbis Images; pp18, 19: Layne Murdoch/NBAE/Getty Images; pp20, 21: Larry W. Smith/EPA/Newscom; pp22, 23: Jason Miller/AP Images; pp24, 25: Chuck Burton/AP Images; pp26, 27: Michael Dwyer/AP Images; pp28, 29: Mark J. Terrill/AP Images; pp30, 31: Ned Dishman/NBAE/Getty Images; p32, top: Andy Lyons/Getty Images; p32, center: D. Clarke Evans/NBAE/Getty Images; p32, bottom: Layne Murdoch Jr./NBAE/Getty Images; p32, background: Jason Miller/AP Images.

Designed by Cheung Tai
Photo Editor: Cynthia Carris

ISBN 978-0-545-80858-3

12 11 10 9 8 7 6 5 4 3 2   15 16 17 18 19 20/0

Printed in the U.S.A.   40
First printing, January 2015

TABLE OF CONTENTS

LAMARCUS ALDRIDGE

FORWARD | PORTLAND TRAIL BLAZERS

HEIGHT: 6' 11" | WEIGHT: 240 LBS | COLLEGE: UNIVERSITY OF TEXAS

Sometimes it takes a great talent to fully develop. That was the case with LaMarcus Aldridge, the Trail Blazers' great power forward. Aldridge was a high school All-American, a top college star, a number two overall draft pick, and a member of the 2007 NBA All-Rookie Team. But it was not until the 2013–14 season that he truly blossomed into one of the NBA's top players. In his eighth season, he posted career-high numbers for points (23.2 per game) and total rebounds (11.1 per game). How did this smart, successful player climb the ladder of success? One step at a time.

Aldridge grew up near Dallas. His older brothers were already star hoopsters. But LaMarcus grew slowly. Through grade school, he was not one of the biggest or strongest kids. He liked basketball, but wasn't really big

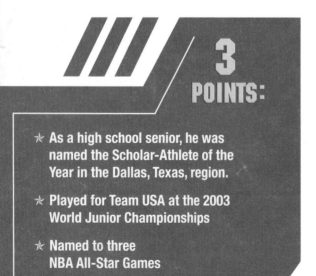

enough to play. That changed by junior high, when he sprouted to 6' 7"!

He began at the University of Texas in 2004 and learned from the older players. His talent couldn't stay on the bench long, though, and he was soon one of the team's top players. Aldridge's inside power game helped the Longhorns reach the Elite Eight at the NCAA tournament. He was named the Big 12's top defender, too.

He joined Portland in 2006. Within a few seasons, he was Portland's "main man," but the team struggled. In 2012, they added young guard Damian Lillard, giving Aldridge the partner he needed. In 2013–14, with Lillard feeding him the ball, Aldridge finally put all the pieces together. He was named to his third All-Star team and made the All-NBA third team. Aldridge's best skills are under the basket, but he is also a fierce defender, often of the opponent's top big man. The kid who couldn't get picked in elementary school has turned out to be the right pick in Portland.

When I Was a kid!
LaMarcus was 6' 7" when he was in eighth grade!

3 POINTS:

⋆ As a high school senior, he was named the Scholar-Athlete of the Year in the Dallas, Texas, region.

⋆ Played for Team USA at the 2003 World Junior Championships

⋆ Named to three NBA All-Star Games

LAMARCUS ALDRIDGE

CARMELO ANTHONY

FORWARD | KNICKS

HEIGHT: 6' 8" | **WEIGHT: 230 LBS** | **COLLEGE: SYRACUSE UNIVERSITY**

In the summer of 2014, millions of fans of the New York Knicks jumped for joy when Carmelo Anthony decided to stay home after he put up another All-Star campaign in 2013–14. They didn't jump as high as he does, however, as one of the NBA's top scoring threats.

Anthony first caught the public's attention when he was named the Most Outstanding Player at the 2003 NCAA Final Four. He led his Syracuse University team to the national championship. Then it was on to the NBA.

After leaving Syracuse after only one year, Anthony spent seven seasons with the Denver Nuggets. He averaged more than 25 points per game over those seasons and earned three All-Star selections while there. Anthony's game is one of multiple moves and a variety of shots. He is one of the rare players who has a deadly outside shot, but also the size and strength to take the ball to the hoop. Opponents have to plan their games around him, often leaving teammates open for their own shots.

Anthony joined the Knicks during the 2011 season and continued his high-scoring ways. With New York, he had 15 games with 40 or more points through 2014. He's been an All-Star four more times with the Knicks. He led the entire NBA in scoring in 2012–13 with 28.7 points per game, which was a career high for him. With that kind of scoring punch, it's no wonder that Knicks fans were so happy with his decision!

Those fans will have even more excitement in 2014–15 when Anthony is joined by new Knicks president Phil Jackson. As a coach, Jackson won an NBA-record 11 championships rings (with the Bulls and Lakers). With talent like Carmelo, he might soon add one as president, too.

When I Was a kid!

To earn a place at the famous Oak Hill Academy, Carmelo had to spend an entire summer taking extra classes. His hard work paid off and he made the school's team!

3 POINTS:

★ Was named to the McDonald's All-America team as a high school senior

★ Was the third freshman ever named Final Four Most Outstanding Player

★ Scored 62 points in 2013-2014 against Charlotte, tops in the NBA that season

CARMELO ANTHONY

STEPHEN CURRY

GUARD | WARRIORS

HEIGHT: 6' 3" | WEIGHT: 185 LBS | COLLEGE: DAVIDSON COLLEGE

From way downtown. Outside the arc. Long-range bomber. Treys. However you talk about three-point shots in the NBA, you have to make sure to include one name: Stephen Curry. The Warriors' All-Star guard is one of the best three-point shooters of all time.

After learning the game from his NBA star dad, Dell Curry, Stephen was a superstar in high school in North Carolina. But he was pretty small for the big-time programs, so he found a home at Davidson College. Pretty soon, no one cared about his size, just about his lights-out shooting skills. Davidson was not one of the elite schools, but thanks in large part to Curry, they reached the "Elite Eight" of the NCAA Tournament in 2009.

When I Was a kid!

Stephen made his first NBA baskets before he got to junior high school. He would practice with his NBA dad, Dell, making buckets at big arenas!

The record-setting guard (see 3 Points) was chosen by the Warriors with the seventh overall pick in the 2009 draft. Except for an injury-shortened 2011–12 season, he's been in their starting lineup ever since. He has led the NBA in three-point field goals in each of the past two seasons, and earned his first All-Star selection in 2014. He was named to the All-NBA second team in 2013–14, his first all-league selection. He was the sixth player ever to top 200 three-pointers in back-to-back seasons.

It's not his genes, though—it's hard work. Curry takes 1,000 shots before every practice. Before games, he shoots from all over the court, making sure to hit shots from each spot. He looks at videos to see how opponents cover him, so his shot is rarely blocked. Want to watch a star in action? Just look downtown.

3 POINTS:

* Set single-season NCAA record with 162 field goals in 2007–08

* It's not just three-pointers: Stephen led the NBA in free-throw percentage in 2010–11

* Set single-season NBA record with 272 three-point field goals in 2012–13

STEPHEN CURRY

ANTHONY DAVIS

FORWARD/CENTER | PELICANS

HEIGHT: 6' 10" | WEIGHT: 220 LBS | COLLEGE: UNIVERSITY OF KENTUCKY

The young players who dominated Anthony Davis on the junior high basketball courts in Chicago will have a story to tell. At the time they were playing against him, Davis was not much more than six feet and had to wear thick glasses while he played. But something happened during high school. Almost overnight, he went from being a 6' 3" guard to a 6' 10" forward with a wingspan that covered the key. No one was going to dominate Davis anymore! Not surprisingly, Davis said at the time, "Being taller made the game much easier!"

Davis was one of the top recruits in the nation after earning national notice in high school. He was also named the nation's top college prospect at the famous NBA Top 100 Camp. He chose to play at the University of

When I Was a kid!

After Anthony shot up in height, his parents had to buy a special king-sized bed so his feet didn't hang over the edge!

Kentucky. Making up for lost time, he used his long arms to become a shot-blocking legend. He blocked 186 shots, setting a school single-season record. Kentucky made it to the NCAA Final Four, and thanks to Davis, the Wildcats won the championship. Davis's defensive domination earned him the Most Outstanding Player Award even though he scored only six points in the championship game.

Anthony wasted no time making his mark on the NBA. After being chosen first overall by the New Orleans Pelicans in the 2012 NBA Draft, he soon proved that they had made the right choice. He played nearly every game and clogged the lane against the NBA's top players. In 2013–14 he led the league with 2.8 blocks per game, and he made players change their shots often. He also led the team with 20.8 points per game, showing his game is more than just D. The Pelicans improved by seven wins, and Davis was a big reason. Look for this wide-winged wonder to become one of the NBA's top big men.

3 POINTS:

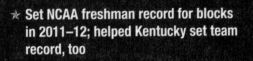

★ Set NCAA freshman record for blocks in 2011–12; helped Kentucky set team record, too

★ Has a wingspan of 7' 4", and he's only 6' 10" himself!

★ In 2014, had fourth-best Player Efficiency Rating in NBA

ANTHONY DAVIS

GORAN DRAGIC

GUARD | SUNS

| HEIGHT: 6' 3" | WEIGHT: 180 LBS | COLLEGE: NONE |

Some fans say that a player who is having a breakout season "came out of nowhere." As Goran Dragic put up the best numbers of his career in early 2014, NBA fans got the word. He was not out of nowhere . . . he was out of Slovenia. That is a nation in central Europe between Italy and Croatia.

Dragic was a pro player by the age of 17 in the Slovenian national basketball league. He played five seasons in Europe, also spending time with a team in Spain. He was doing very well, but he wanted to test his game against the best players in the world, so he went into the 2008 NBA Draft.

The Suns chose him in the second round and he found a role as bench player. With star guard Steve Nash running the offense, Dragic was a backup. He started fewer than 10 games in each of his first four seasons. After he was traded to Houston during the 2010–11 season, he returned to the Suns for 2011–12. He finally earned a starting job in 2012 when Nash moved to the Lakers. Dragic responded with a solid 14.7 points per game.

His 2013–14 season was moving along fine when he suddenly erupted in January. Over the course of the next several months, he set several new career points-per-game marks, while leading the Suns' offense. His best game was 40 points on February 28.

When I Was a kid!

There was no NBA.com for young Goran. If he wanted to watch NBA games live on Slovenian TV, he had to wake up at two in the morning!

Even though Dragic averaged 20.3 points per game, the Suns couldn't make the playoffs in a tight Western Conference race. They are only the second team ever to win 48 games and not make the postseason!

Because of Goran's leadership and skills, he was named the NBA's Most Improved Player. He also made the All-NBA third team. Dragic is not a mystery anymore!

3 POINTS:

* Won gold medal with Slovenia at 2003 World Under-20 Championship

* Had nine 30-plus point games in 2013–14; had only three in previous five seasons

* Name is pronounced GORE-un DRAG-itch

GORAN DRAGIC

TIM DUNCAN

FORWARD/CENTER | SPURS

HEIGHT: 6' 11" | **WEIGHT: 248 LBS** | **COLLEGE: WAKE FOREST UNIVERSITY**

Just when NBA opponents thought he might be done, the legendary Tim Duncan showed he had more gas in the tank. Duncan led the Spurs to their fifth NBA championship in 2014. Before Duncan arrived, the Spurs had zero titles. Since he joined them in 1997, they have five in his 17 seasons. In fact, they have made the playoffs every year he has been on the team.

Duncan is so humble, however, that he'd be the first to point to his outstanding teammates. But he is the glue that holds the Spurs' super system together.

Duncan has only led the NBA in one major category—rebounds in 2002. He could probably win scoring titles and rebounding titles every year, but he knows that by playing as a team, the Spurs will win. The experts know how great he is, however. Duncan has been named to the All-NBA first team 10 times. He was the NBA Most Valuable Player in 2002 and 2003, as well as a three-time NBA Finals MVP.

Duncan showed that he was still among the best after the Spurs were shocked late in the 2013 NBA Finals by the Heat. They had a big lead but lost when the Heat came back. But Duncan rallied his team to return to the Finals and avenge that stunning loss. They finished 2013–14 with the NBA's best regular-season record. After slipping past Dallas, they rolled through the playoffs.

In the Finals, they met the Heat again and this time it was no contest. The Spurs simply dominated. In each of their four wins (they only lost once), they beat Miami by at least 15 points! More bad news for rival NBA teams: Duncan is coming back for more!

3 POINTS:

- ★ At Wake Forest, was named college player of the year in 1997
- ★ Named to NBA All-Defensive First Team eight times
- ★ Has blocked more shots than any player currently in the NBA; is seventh all-time in that category

When I Was a kid!

Tim grew up in the US Virgin Islands. He was all set to become a champion swimmer but when he grew so much, he tried basketball instead!

TIM DUNCAN

KEVIN DURANT

FORWARD | THUNDER

HEIGHT: 6' 9" | WEIGHT: 215 LBS | COLLEGE: UNIVERSITY OF TEXAS

Well, it had to happen one of these years. Kevin Durant could have won numerous MVP awards if it were not for a guy named LeBron James. Durant won three straight NBA scoring titles, but finished behind James in the MVP voting. His team, the Oklahoma City Thunder, also finished behind the Heat in the race for NBA titles, too. While Durant is still chasing that championship ring, he now has his own MVP trophy.

The long, tall, shooting machine won his fourth scoring title with a career-best 32.0 points-per-game average. He also led the NBA in field goals made and attempted. Even when opponents try to foul him to slow down his scoring, he pumps in free throws 87 percent of the time! (He even led the league in free-throw percentage in 2012–13!)

Durant's scoring skills are no surprise. He was a superstar in high school in Maryland and then at the University of Texas. After just one college season, he moved to the NBA. With the Seattle SuperSonics, he was the NBA Rookie of the Year. After the team moved to Oklahoma City, their new team name—the Thunder—described the power Durant used on the court. His long arms and quick moves make him dangerous in the paint. But it's his deadly outside shooting that really sets him apart from other big men.

When I Was a kid!

Kevin was a national champion when he was 11! His AAU team, the Prince George Jaguars, won the national title when he scored 18 points in the final!

He scored off the court, too, with his great acceptance speech for the MVP. He tearfully thanked his mom and his family for supporting him throughout his career. He thanked his coaches, his teammates, and even the team trainer!

With the MVP goal accomplished, Durant and the Thunder have one more goal to reach: hoisting that championship banner in Oklahoma City!

3 POINTS:

* Won both Naismith and Wooden awards as 2007 college player of the year

* Has led the NBA in points scored four seasons since 2009–10

* Has been named to NBA All-Star Game five times

KEVIN DURANT

BLAKE GRIFFIN

FORWARD | CLIPPERS

| HEIGHT: 6' 10" | WEIGHT: 251 LBS | COLLEGE: UNIVERSITY OF OKLAHOMA |

You probably know about Blake Griffin's amazing ability to dunk. He is one of the NBA's most powerful players, able to rise above the crowd and slam home the ball from almost any angle. But in the past two seasons, he has worked hard to show that he is more than just a dunking machine. By working on his all-around game, Griffin has become more than just a dunker . . . he has become a player.

Griffin rode his slammin' success through his high school years in Oklahoma, where he won four state championships. Though colleges around the country wanted him to travel to play for them, he decided to stay home. Blake played two seasons for the University of Oklahoma Sooners and won several national player-of-the-year honors.

When you are a college superstar, chances are you'll be drafted by a lower-ranked NBA team. That's because teams with the worst records draft first. The Los Angeles Clippers took Blake with the first overall pick in 2009. That might have doomed him to years in the NBA basement, but he had other ideas. After missing what would have been his first season with a knee injury, he rebounded to win the 2011 NBA Rookie of the Year award.

The Clippers had also gotten Blake some help, adding all-everything point guard Chris Paul. Now Blake did not have to depend on dunks. He upped his defense, he worked on his outside shooting, and he continued to dominate the offensive and defensive boards. By 2013, the Clippers won more games than in any season in their history! In 2014, they set another team record for wins while also leading the NBA in team scoring. Plus, Blake had a career-high scoring average (24.1 ppg). With his status as an NBA leading man and dunking star established, Blake still has one more title to shoot for: NBA champion.

When I Was a kid!

Many of the trophies that Blake won as a superstar young athlete were already part of the "family." His parents ran a trophy-making business.

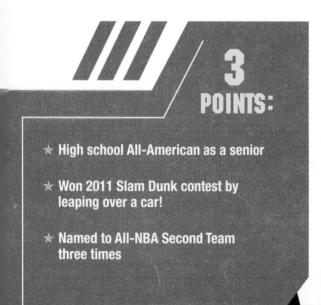

3 POINTS:

★ High school All-American as a senior

★ Won 2011 Slam Dunk contest by leaping over a car!

★ Named to All-NBA Second Team three times

18

BLAKE GRIFFIN

DWIGHT HOWARD

FORWARD/CENTER | ROCKETS

HEIGHT: 6' 11" | **WEIGHT: 240 LBS** | **COLLEGE: NONE**

Lakers fans did not enjoy the 2013–14 season. One big reason was that their team was having one of its worst seasons since 1960. Another was that one of their former players was tearing it up—for another club! Dwight Howard has been a dominant force no matter where he has played. He was with the Lakers in 2012–13 after eight awesome seasons in Orlando. In 2013–14, he helped Houston "rocket" to the playoffs with his glass-cleaning, paint-dominating style.

Howard was one of the few NBA players to make the jump right from high school to the pros. New rules put in place mean that he might be one of the last. At Southwest Atlanta Christian Academy, he helped his team win the state title. But he won just about every national award there was to win. Instead of college, he chose the NBA. He was the first overall pick of the 2004 NBA Draft by the Orlando Magic.

Howard quickly showed that he had made the right move. He led the NBA in total rebounds in 2005 when he was only 20 years old. He was the youngest ever to be tops in that stat. Over the next few seasons, he established himself as the last guy any opponent wanted to see on the floor. He won three straight NBA Defensive Player of the Year Awards (2008–10) and twice led the league in blocks per game.

Howard turned the Magic around, leading them to the playoffs five straight seasons starting in 2007. They got as far as the 2009 NBA Finals, though they lost there to the Lakers.

One of Howard's most memorable career moments came in the 2008 NBA Dunk Contest. For his final dunk, he wore a big *S* on his chest and even tied on a cape. After his final slam won the contest, he had won a new nickname, too: Superman!

When I Was a kid!

In a seventh-grade essay, Dwight predicted that he would be the top pick in the NBA Draft!

3 POINTS:

* Named 2004 McDonald's All-American as a high school senior and also sang in the school choir

* Has led NBA in total rebounds six times

* Named to eight NBA All-Star Games

DWIGHT HOWARD

LEBRON JAMES

FORWARD | CAVALIERS

| HEIGHT: 6' 8" | WEIGHT: 240 LBS | COLLEGE: NONE |

Y ou watch LeBron James now and you see an amazing athlete. He has unmatched basketball skills, a shelf full of awards (including four NBA MVP trophies), and a pair of NBA championship rings. He's a 10-time All-Star. But the veteran superstar with 14 million Twitter followers started out rough. He and his mom moved from house to house for several years, with LeBron often carrying all he owned in a little blue backpack.

Sports became his way out, first with football and then basketball. Through sports, he connected with other families who helped him. In fact, he even moved in with one of those families for a while. For the first time in his life, he had stability. He learned to work hard to make his natural skills even better.

By the time he was a sophomore in high school, he was the best basketball player in Ohio. Two years later, he was nationally famous as the best young player in the nation.

When I Was a kid!

LeBron's first favorite sport was football. He won the job of running back by winning a sprinting race. Then, on his first carry, he ran 80 yards for a touchdown!

In 2003, he was the number one draft pick in the NBA. Along with his contract with the Cleveland Cavaliers, he signed up to endorse several products. The kid who didn't really have a home suddenly was making $100 million a year.

All the hype and the money didn't change his game. He quickly moved into the top rank of players, showing off scoring power and amazing moves, plus veteran leadership from a young player. He became simply "The King."

After seven amazing seasons with Cleveland, he made a big move to the Miami Heat. There he teamed with Dwyane Wade and Chris Bosh to form "The Big Three." Together, they went to four straight NBA Finals, winning it all in 2012 and 2013. In 2014, however, he made millions of Ohio hoops fans happy by "coming home" to the Cavaliers. He even took back his old No. 23 jersey.

Few athletes have been as successful as James. Few have had a tougher beginning. From great struggles can come great success.

3 POINTS:

★ 2004 NBA Rookie of the Year

★ Helped US win 2008 Olympic gold medal

★ Has won an amazing 45 NBA Player of the Week awards

LEBRON JAMES

AL JEFFERSON

CENTER | HORNETS

HEIGHT: 6' 10" | **WEIGHT: 265 LBS** | **COLLEGE: NONE**

Sometimes a player just needs to find the right home to thrive. Al Jefferson had been a solid player for almost a decade, but he had never found the right place to use his many talents. After landing in Charlotte, however, he had the best season of his career, earning All-NBA third-team honors. Though he is still looking for his first All-Star Game selection, Jefferson has found a home.

After averaging 42 points a game as a high school senior in Mississippi, Jefferson started his NBA career without going to college. The Boston Celtics chose him with the 15th pick of the 2004 NBA Draft. Jefferson's early NBA seasons were disappointing. Several injuries slowed his progress, plus he also had to have his appendix taken out! After three years in Boston, he was traded to the Minnesota Timberwolves. Once again, he played well, but was not a star, though he did have a career-high 23.1 points per game average in 2008–09. However, a knee injury cost him part of that season, too.

Minnesota was not home, either, and he was traded to the Utah Jazz in 2010. Again, he was fine, averaging about 18 points per game in three seasons, but never really shining. Then it was on to Charlotte.

Jefferson found that he fit into the Bobcats' system perfectly. They focused on defense, and he had the teammates around him to be the main man on offense, too. He really came on toward the end of the season, winning back-to-back Eastern Conference Player of the Month awards. Charlotte made the playoffs for the first time since 2010, but they were swept by the Miami Heat. The team loved his work so much, they bought a big ad in the Charlotte newspaper just to say thanks!

After several years as the Bobcats, Charlotte will change their name to the Hornets this season. Jefferson will have another fresh start at getting into the postseason.

When I Was a kid!

When Al was in high school, he attended a camp run by Michael Jordan. He got to play with Jordan . . . and MJ fed Big Al with a perfect alley-oop pass for a dunk!

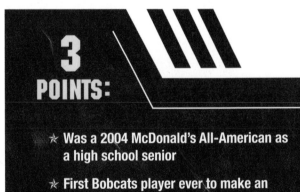

3 POINTS:

* Was a 2004 McDonald's All-American as a high school senior

* First Bobcats player ever to make an All-NBA team

* Mr. Dependable: has played at least 59 games in every NBA season except one

AL JEFFERSON

JOAKIM NOAH

CENTER | BULLS

HEIGHT: 6' 11" | **WEIGHT: 232 LBS** | **COLLEGE: UNIVERSITY OF FLORIDA**

Joakim Noah has covered a lot of miles to make it to the top in the NBA. His latest trips have been just 94 feet (the length of a court), however, but they have been his most important. The globetrotting Frenchman has turned from basketball's "free spirit" to one of the NBA's best players.

Noah grew up in France. His father, Yannick, was a tennis champion—he won the 1983 French Open, among his 23 pro-tournament titles. Joakim chose basketball, however. One reason was that he was quickly growing too tall for tennis. The other was to do something different from his dad. They moved to New York City when he was 12, and he quickly became one of the top players in the area.

At the University of Florida, he was part of back-to-back national-championship teams. Noah, in fact, was the Most Outstanding Player of the Final Four in Florida's first title run. The Chicago Bulls made him the ninth overall pick in the 2007 Draft.

Noah found that his easygoing, curious personality drew attention. Few NBA players speak the languages he can, or have as much interest in travel, the arts, and culture. He regularly makes trips to Africa, China, and Europe.

However, on the court, he has shown the intensity that he avoids off the court. For his first few NBA seasons, the Bulls were led by guard Derrick Rose. Noah's job was to clog the lane and feed the ball to Rose. But in 2013 and 2014, Rose missed most of both seasons with injuries. With Rose gone, the focus of Chicago's game plan turned to the big man. By the end of 2014, he was still dominating on the boards, but also playing a big role on offense. From 2007 to 2013, Noah had just two games with 10 or more assists. In 2013–14, he had eight. He has become one of the best-passing big men in the NBA.

When I Was a kid!

Though he grew up in Paris, Noah went to an "American" school that had basketball. As he grew up, his mom would have to drive farther and farther to find gyms for him to play in . . . hoops was not a big deal in France!

3 POINTS:

- ★ Two-time NBA All-Star
- ★ Through 2013–14, Noah was still looking for his first successful three-point shot!
- ★ Had 14 assists in a game in March 2014; most in a game by an NBA center since 1986

JOAKIM NOAH

CHRIS PAUL

GUARD | CLIPPERS

| HEIGHT: 6' 0" | WEIGHT: 175 LBS | COLLEGE: WAKE FOREST UNIVERSITY |

If the definition of "most valuable" is how much a player helps his team improve, then Chris Paul should have three MVP trophies. As it is, he's happy with how he has helped turn the Los Angeles Clippers around. From the second-best team in the country's second-biggest city, the Clips have become one of the most feared teams in the West! Paul's dazzling passing game and fast-hands defense have combined with power forward Blake Griffin's inside game to transform the Clippers into contenders.

Paul grew up in North Carolina. Though football was his favorite sport as a kid, by high school, he had moved to hoops. Good move! As a senior, he averaged 30.8 points and eight assists per game. He was an All-American and named the top player in his basketball-crazy state.

When I Was a kid!

Chris got his first basketball hoop when he was three. It was a plastic toy hung in his basement. His brother made a court by putting tape on the floor!

He stayed near home for college, attending Wake Forest. He was the ACC Rookie of the Year as a freshman, then helped a US junior team win the 2004 World Junior Tournament. He helped the Demon Deacons reach the second round of the NCAA tournament again. Next up: the NBA!

The Hornets made him the fourth overall pick and he played so well he was named the NBA Rookie of the Year. The Hornets went all the way to Game 7 of the second round, one of their best performances ever. He led them to the playoffs twice more. In 2011, however, he was traded to the Clippers. Talk about good moves!

In Paul's first year in L.A., the team reached the playoffs for the first time since 2006. In 2013–14, they were the highest-scoring team in the NBA and their 57 wins were the most in team history. Once Paul and Griffin can figure out the playoffs, look for a ring on this awesome guard's finger.

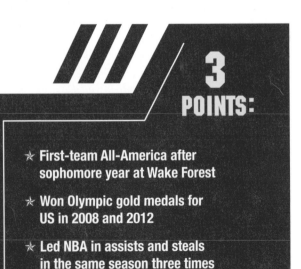

3 POINTS:

- ★ First-team All-America after sophomore year at Wake Forest
- ★ Won Olympic gold medals for US in 2008 and 2012
- ★ Led NBA in assists and steals in the same season three times

CHRIS PAUL

JOHN WALL

GUARD | WIZARDS

HEIGHT: 6' 4" | WEIGHT: 195 LBS | COLLEGE: UNIVERSITY OF KENTUCKY

When the Ping-Pong ball bounced the right way for the Washington Wizards before the 2010 NBA Draft, they had the easiest pick in years. Kentucky's slashing guard John Wall was clearly the best player out there. So the Wizards must have waved their wand and come up lucky.

Wall's early life growing up in North Carolina was not so lucky. His father died when Wall was just eight years old. Young Wall found his strength in sports. He played with top local AAU teams and the coaches tried to help him grow off the court, too. By the time he finished high school, he was one of the top players in the country.

Wall chose to play at Kentucky, where Coach John Calipari ran an offense that could use Wall's slashing, driving, speedy style. Wall combined with a talented group of young players to help Kentucky win the SEC title. Wall was the SEC Tournament MVP and later was named a first-team All-American, a rare honor for a freshman.

Wall was so good that he was ready for the NBA . . . and the NBA couldn't wait.

Teams that finish in the bottom seven earn a shot at the top draft pick. The commissioner chooses them at random from a lottery machine. Washington came up the winner.

Wall was not a superstar from the start, however. He had to adjust his skills to the NBA's faster, stronger game. But over his first couple of seasons, he made big steps each year. In 2013–14, he put it all together, earning his first All-Star Game selection and leading the NBA in total assists. Even bigger news was that he led the Wizards to their first playoff series since 2008 and first playoff series win (over Chicago) since 2005! Wall fits the Wizards—he makes magic!

When I Was a kid!

John was such a rebel when he was young he was actually cut from the varsity team at one high school. But he learned from that and bounced back to become a star!

3 POINTS:

* Finalist for 2009 John Wooden Award as top college player

* Had a triple-double in only his ninth NBA game (2009)

* Member of the 2010–11 NBA All-Rookie Team

JOHN WALL

KAWHI LEONARD

The San Antonio Spurs are packed with stars, including Tim Duncan, Tony Parker, and Manu Ginobili. But when they won their fifth NBA title in 2014, none of these stars were the Finals MVP. That honor went to the next big Spurs star, Kawhi (kah-WHY) Leonard. In only his third season, Leonard started nearly every game as small forward opposite Duncan. When the Heat collapsed on the "Big Three," the Spurs coach, Gregg Popovich turned to his secret weapon. Leonard scored 29, 20, and 22 points in Games 3, 4, and 5 to help the Spurs clinch the title.

MICHAEL CARTER-WILLIAMS

In 2013–14, Philadelphia guard Michael Carter-Williams was the NBA Rookie of the Year. Now can he follow up by becoming one of the best NBA players overall? Carter-Williams led all NBA first-year players in points, rebounds, and assists. He was only the third rookie ever to do so and the first since Alvan Adams in 1976. He sure got off to a hot start, scoring 22 points in his first game as the Sixers beat the mighty Heat.

DAMIAN LILLARD

Lillard played college hoops at tiny Weber State in Utah. But he was discovered by Portland and burst onto the NBA in 2012–13. Lillard surprised many by becoming the NBA Rookie of the Year that season. His pinpoint passing and shooting touch have helped turn Portland into a contender. As a rookie, he started every one of the team's 82 games, and also led the league in minutes played, a rare feat. In his second season, Lillard and the Trail Blazers made the Western Conference finals for the first time since 2000.